ch

ds &
etters
13

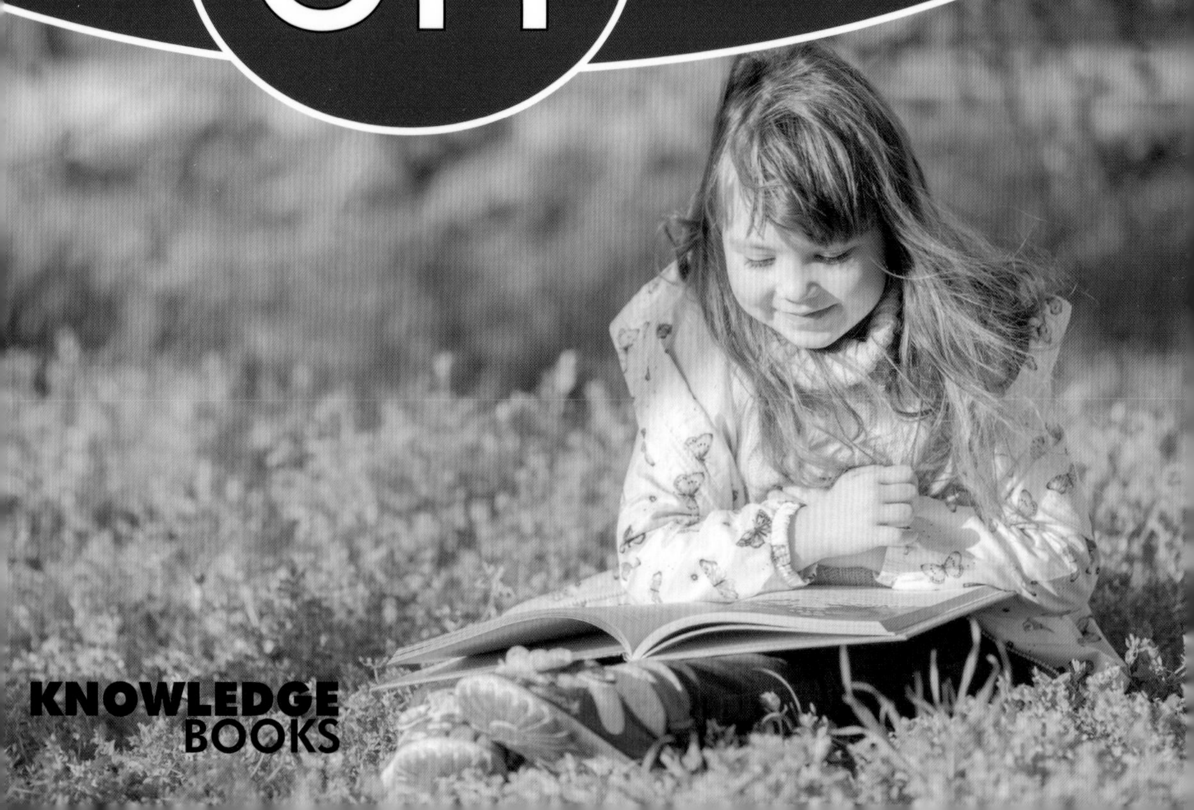

KNOWLEDGE
BOOKS

cheese	church
chess	chick
chair	chain
cherry	

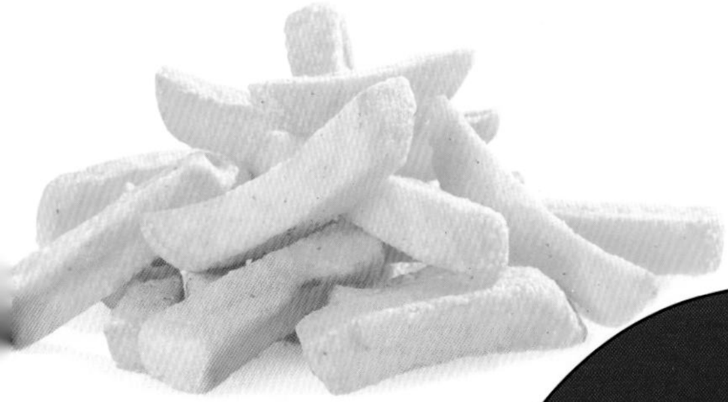

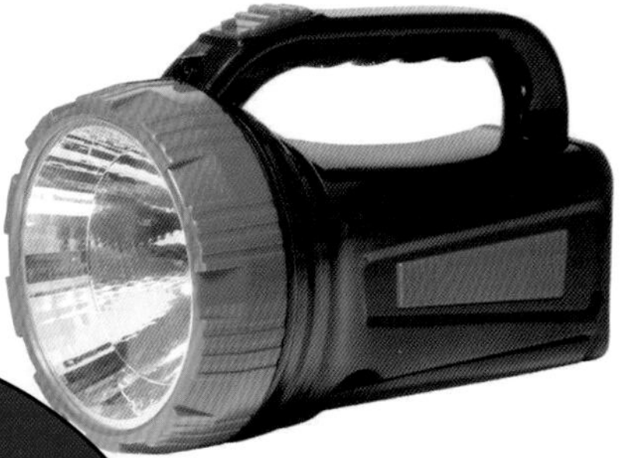

ch

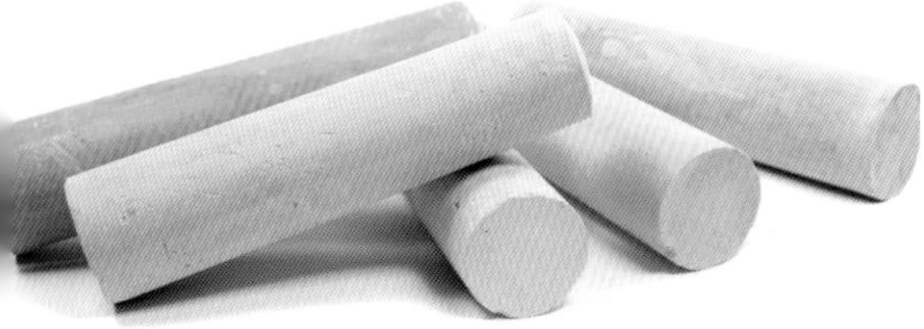

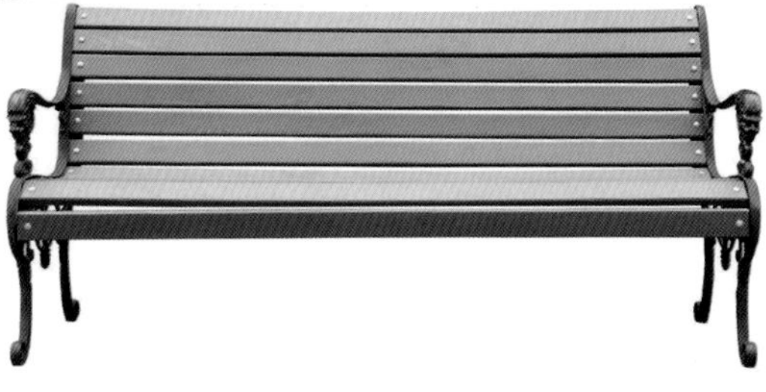

cheese

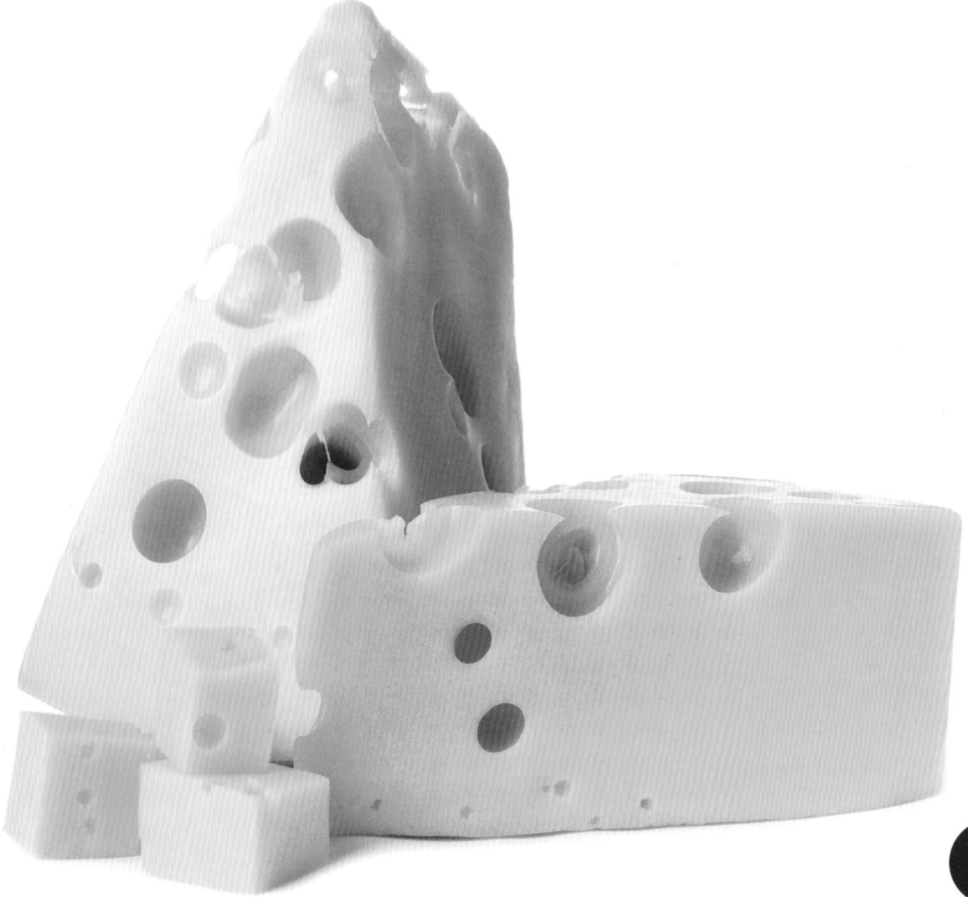

church

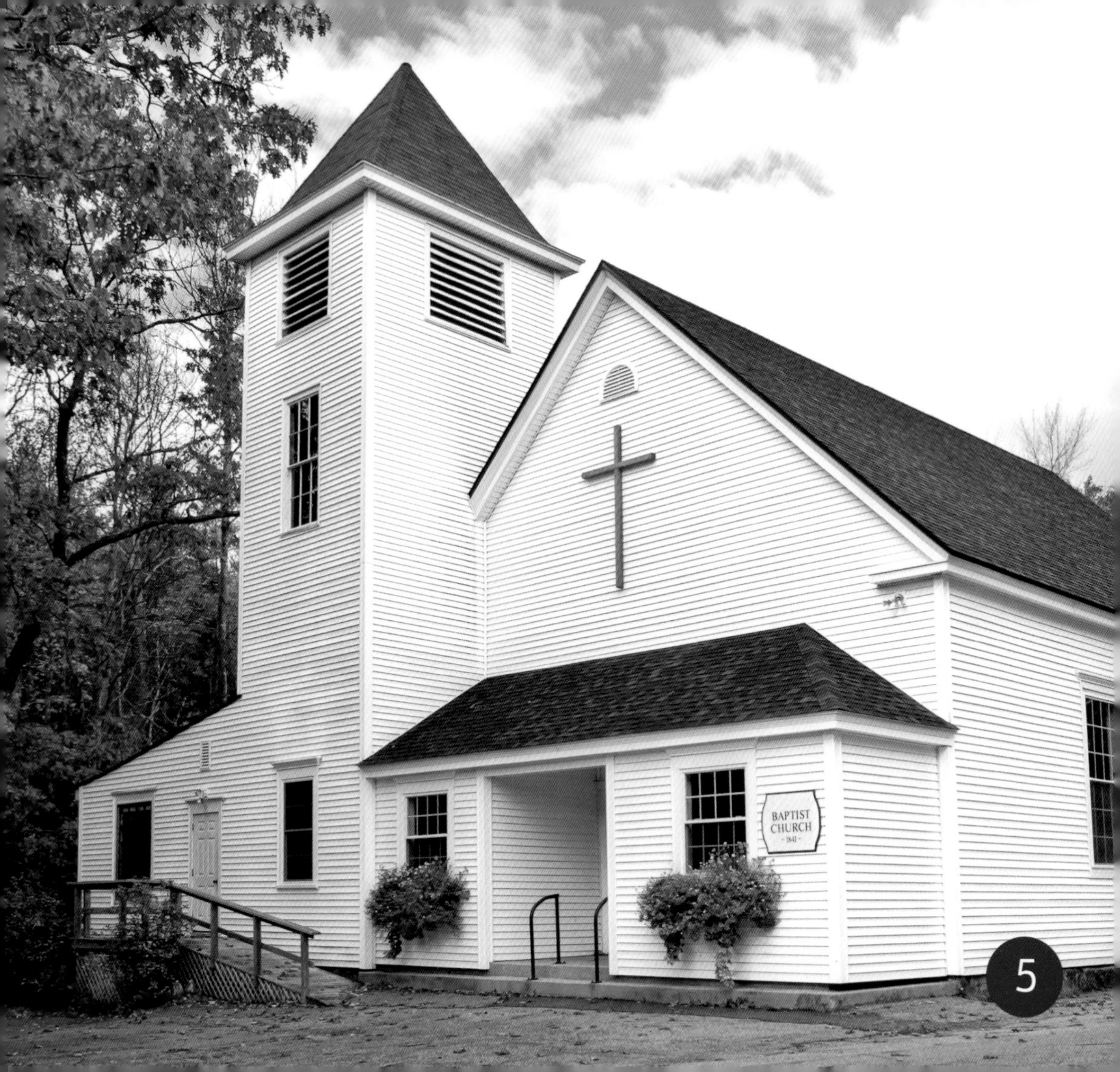
BAPTIST
CHURCH
1841
5

chess

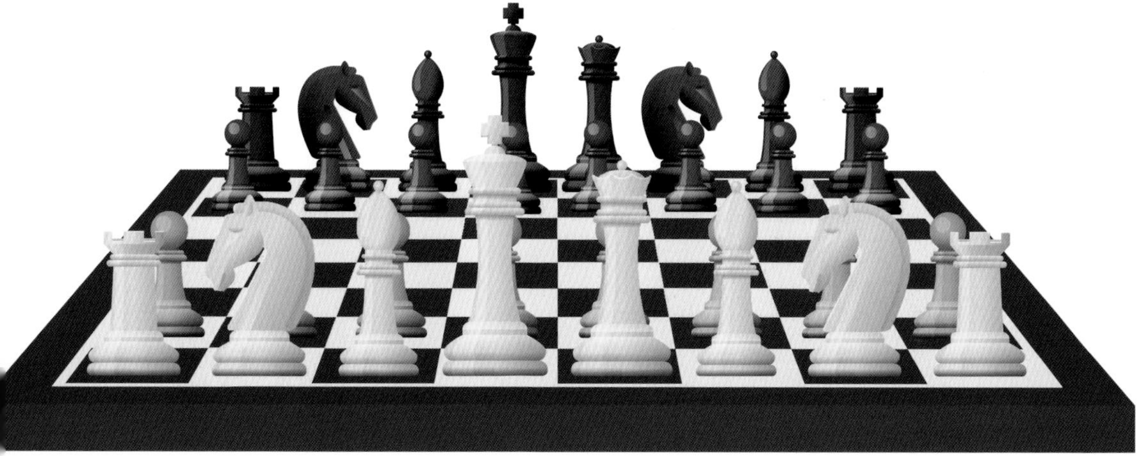

chick

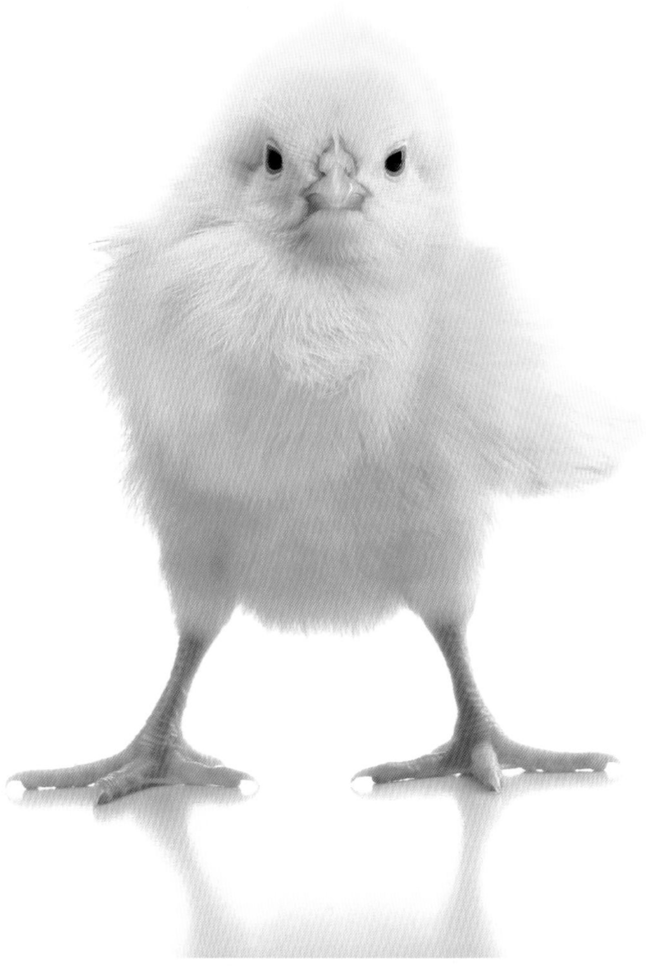

chair

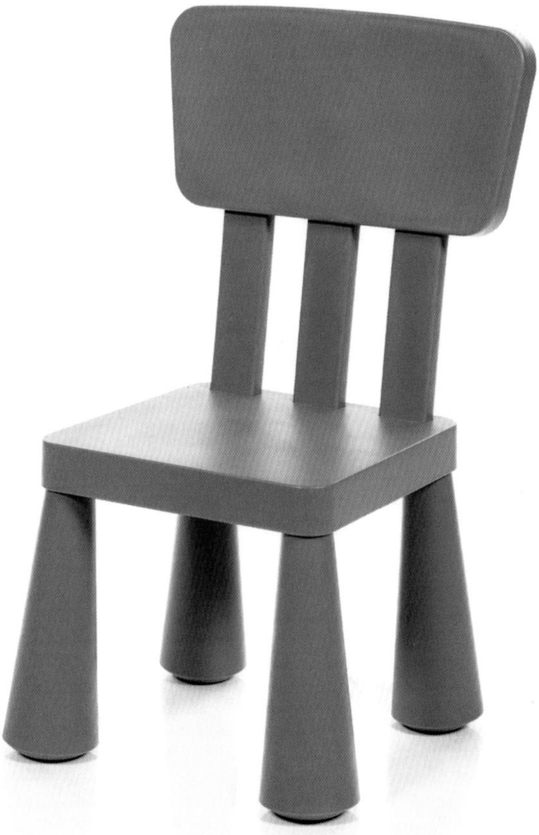

chain

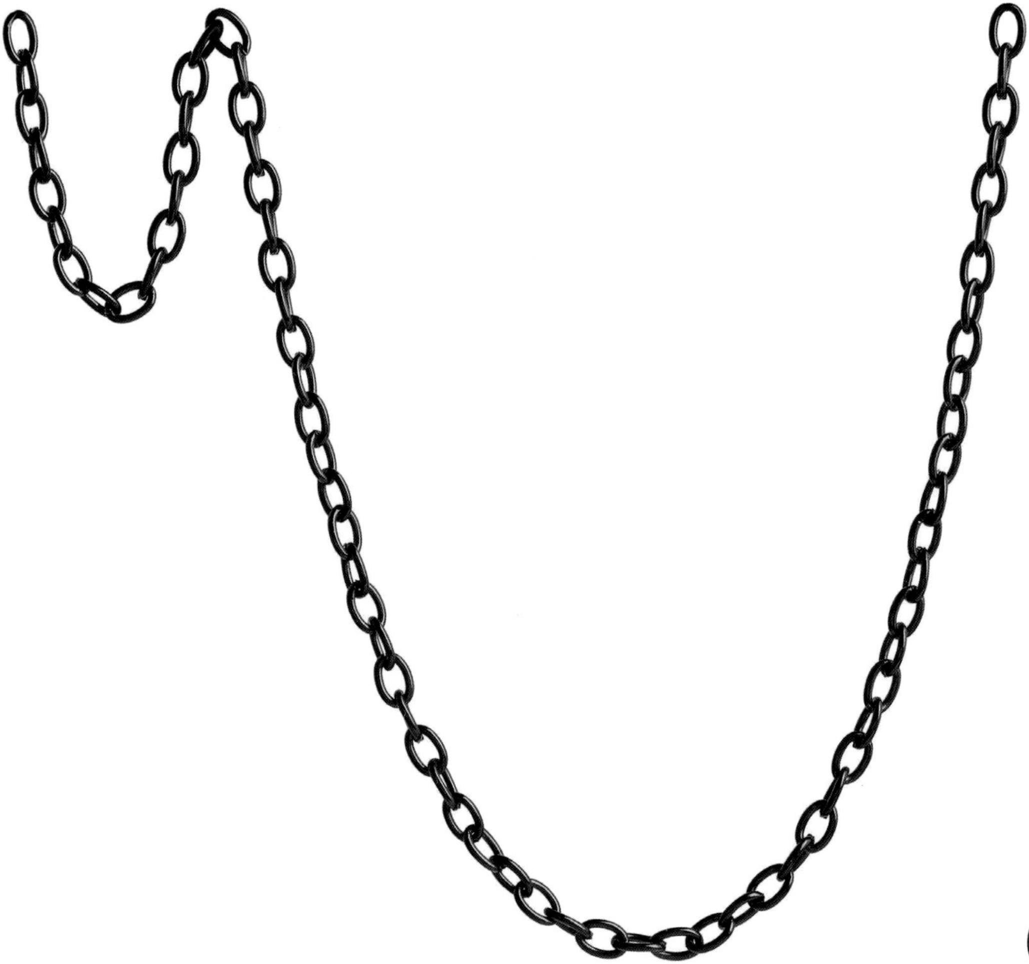

cherry

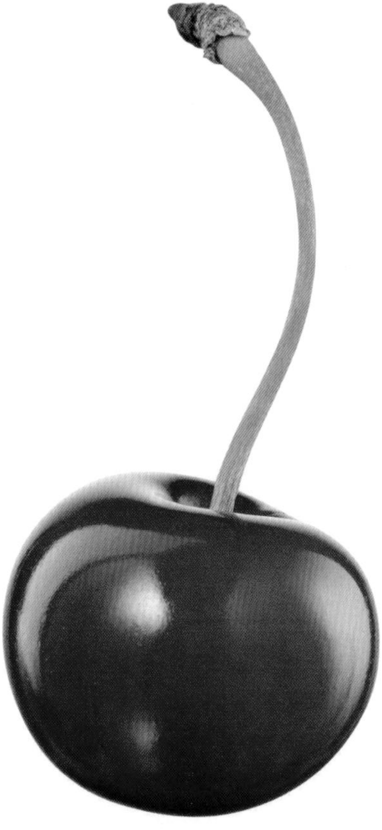

cheese	church
chess	chick
chair	chain
cherry	